Blessings of Peace

100 Meditations
Inspired by the Writings of
Judaism, Christianity and Islam.

Jonti Marks

Copyright Notice:

First published in 2024 by Jonti Marks
(KPD print book ISBN 9798882979231)
© Jonti Marks 2024

All rights reserved. No part of this publication may be reproduced, distributed, or transmitted in any form or by any means, including photocopying, recording, or other electronic or mechanical methods, without the prior written permission of the author, except in the case of brief quotations embodied in critical reviews and certain other non-commercial uses permitted by copyright law.

For permission requests please write to the author at: jonti.marks@gmail.com

For more information, please visit:
www.jontimarks.com

Introduction.

This book was written as a personal response to the uprush of feelings provoked by the current state of the world.

It is February 2024. As I write, the war between Ukraine and Russia rumbles on into its third year. In the Middle-East, Israel continues its bombardment of Gaza, and every day, in these conflicts and others, people are suffering and dying.

Sea levels rise, weather patterns change – and as a result, people are dying. In a world of plenty, famine, that most grisly of the four horsemen, is still free to stalk the lands and, in pitiful and always avoidable circumstances, people continue to die.

It is so hard to maintain a balance through all of this. How does a person who believes in God and in the Brotherhood/Sisterhood of all mankind approach these crises? How do we find a point of reference that allows us to make a stand for a more just and caring world? How do we stay sane in a world gone mad? When so many of our former certainties are certain no longer, where can we find a firm rock on which to stand? With so many clamouring for an audience, with so many arguing for this philosophy or that, how do we find a voice that cuts through to the core of all problems and speaks with love and understanding for all?

For me, the only way to make sense of anything is to take a longer view; to zoom out a little and try to see things with a greater perspective. That may sound cold, and it is true that a level of detachment is the result. However, it is also the case that, in adopting such a perspective, we acknowledge the truth of our interconnectedness and thus we put ourselves right back into the heart of the suffering, this time without any sense of partisanship or partiality, but only with compassion and, it must be said, a weight of sorrow.

On my laptop, I have a picture with a quotation, ironically, given the focus of this book, from the Bhagavad-Gita. It says: "Never was there a time when I did not exist, nor you, nor all these kings; nor in the future will any of us cease to be." It is an idea that certainly puts things in a particular perspective and allows for a certain amount of detachment. But I feel it would be wrong to allow that rather lofty, almost impersonal attitude to be the only one with which we face things.

Yes, we can say that, from a cosmic perspective, none of this is very significant. In the light of eternity, the here and now means little, but, on the other hand, here and now is all we have: we are caught up in a dance of interaction where what we do and how we relate to each other is important and does matter.

I believe that we are in essence spiritual beings living temporarily in physical bodies and so, while it may be true that war and hunger, disease and death, pain and suffering do not touch the 'real' us, there is still an imperative to relieve the suffering of others, however transitory or illusory one may believe it to be.

As spiritual beings, I believe we are here to embody and manifest the oneness of the Universe; we are here to be the means by which the Universe evolves towards the Godhead. And, for me at least, the way to do this is to learn and practise love. That love starts with self-knowledge: to find God within our own hearts, and from there, this knowledge leads us to the understanding that God resides in the heart of all and, indeed, in every atom of Creation. What else can it mean to be omnipresent?

And so I find that I hold fast to my belief that all is well and, at the same time, I do what I can to help make things better. This book is one such attempt. I hope you find something of value in it and that, together, in tiny increments, we might be able to help bring about a world that is full of justice and peace and love.

A Word

I would like to acknowledge the fact that any use of the word 'God' is difficult. It is loaded and overloaded with preconceptions. I use it because it is the most convenient word we have in English for the concept of a Supreme Being. I use it, as far as possible, without wanting to define it, and I urge you to understand it in your own terms. I have attached the masculine pronouns to it because that is the convention.

In labelling and identifying the quotations, I have been as accurate as I can. Where the source is given as a document, I have referenced that document. Where a quotation is attributed to a particular person, I have given their name, but not necessarily the book (or whatever) from which it comes.

Quotations from the Bible tend to have the book title, chapter and verse number. Quotations from other Sacred Volumes are often a bit more vague although I have given as much detail as I can. I apologise if this causes any difficulty, but given the huge range of translations and interpretations available, it is not always easy for an 'outsider' such as myself to be accurate. I feel that inaccuracy or error would be worse than vagueness. If any such errors exist, I apologise without reservation. No disrespect is intended.

JAM
Feb 2024

Dedication

To my dear Brother,
Marcus Hill, whose constant greeting
gave me the title for this book;
to my dear friend, Shuli Oded,
who was ever in my thoughts as I wrote;
to Lucy Lepchani,
who fights so fiercely
and speaks so eloquently
for what is right;
and to Jo, always,
for love and support
beyond measure.

"Spread the greeting of peace among yourselves."
Hadith, Sahih Muslim

To put peace first in our lives is to open ourselves up to trust, togetherness and love. To greet each person with the blessing of peace is to establish, from the very outset of every interaction, a benevolent and selfless foundation for our relationships.

But the blessing of peace can be extended even further. Imagine if we were to greet each day with the promise of peace, not only in our dealings with others, but also for ourselves and for the whole world.

Imagine a relationship founded on the principles of true peace with ourselves, each other, our fellow creatures and with our whole environment. Imagine what it would be like to establish such a relationship with the rivers and seas, with the earth and the sky.

Like yeast in dough, such a blessing works quietly, from heart to heart, until the whole world is filled with it; until each person feels it; until the earth itself is healed and whole.

Let us determine to offer this great gift to ourselves and each other every day. It is not always easy – we are so often thwarted by personal considerations and our apparent differences – but we can practise. We can make the effort, every day, to live in the light of this blessing and thus remember that we are all part of one life, given by God.

"Love your neighbour as yourself."
Leviticus 19:18

To love our neighbour as ourselves, we must first learn to love ourselves. But what does this mean?

We all have faults and we have all done things that we regret. We can all feel remorse, shame or guilt, but these things are personality-based. If we have faults, they are rooted in our character which, in turn, is determined by our background and upbringing.

True self-love is rooted in something else. It is based on the understanding that, metaphorically at least, we are created in the image of God, and that our true and deepest selves are spiritual and even divine in nature.

So self-love is not about the ego. Quite the opposite – to love ourselves is to recognise the spark of divinity that resides in every heart. It is to acknowledge that it resides equally in the heart of all living beings and it is what connects us all as brothers and sisters.

Life is God's greatest gift, and our task is to love and honour it, to uphold and support it, recognising it as the means whereby we may come back to our Creator. When we understand that the same life is present in all, barriers come down and we are able to blossom into the life of peace and love that is our birthright.

"A new command I give you: Love one another. As I have loved you, so you must love one another."
John 13:34

God's love is given to us unconditionally. It is not a result of what we do but of what we are. When we come to fully appreciate and accept such boundless love, we are more able to share it with others.

In this fragmented world in which we live, it is vital for us to be able to accept differences in each other without feeling threatened by them.

Fear is the great separator of people, the greatest threat to all of our well-being, all of our peace, all of our prosperity. It robs us of the ability to see the similarities that underlie our differences. It prevents us from recognising the divine in each other and in ourselves. It is the root and source of the voice that tells us that we are under threat, the voice that tells us to attack first, to take revenge, to seek to obliterate and destroy.

Everything that God wants from us, everything that He asks of us; everything that He offers us - all is encapsulated in this injunction to love.

Love is the force that lets us lower our guard and see each other for what we truly are. It is peace, and freedom from fear. It is our foundation and our essence; the rock upon which justice is built, the primary building block for the world we all wish to see and believe is possible.

"And He is with you wherever you are."

Quran 57:4

Each of us carries within ourselves a spark of the Divine life. It is what animates us, and it is what we truly are.

Beyond the illusion of body and mind, of ego and self, there lies, quiet and unchanging, our true and highest self. And within that highest self - that spirit soul - is God himself, separate but the same. Just as a drop of the ocean has all the properties of the vastness from which it came but is not that vastness; or as a spark from a fire is bright and hot but is not the whole fire - so our souls are, in essence, of God but they are not God.

But God is near - so close, within us, so much a part of us. Always there, always available, always waiting for us to be still and listen.

And if He lies within our heart, must He not also be within the heart of others? When we look at another human being, how would it be if we trained ourselves to see, not just a body, not just a physical identity, but to see God incarnate? How would it be if we could look beyond all outer forms and see the truth that lies within? And seeing it, how could we fight? How could we wage war if we understood that we battle against ourselves and against God Himself.

God is close. He never leaves us. Neither does His love.

"Greater is the one who does a mitzvah (good deed) through others than the one who does it alone."
Talmud, Kiddushin 39b

The more we can learn to bring others into our circle, the sooner we can create communities of caring and like-minded individuals. We don't need to rest within the community boundaries that the world sets for us, we are free to seek out those with whom we resonate and with whom we are able to be our best selves.

Once we decide to rise above self-interest and do good in the world, we naturally attract and are attracted to those who wish to do the same.

To do good quietly and alone is fine, but to act together and do good together is incrementally more powerful. To break down divisions of race and class, religion and culture, age and gender, and find, beyond worldly labels, a disinterested commonality of benevolence and love is, clearly, best of all.

And to provide opportunities for others to experience the joy and freedom which are found in service to the general good is to give a manifold gift to the world. It adds to both the general good and to the well-being of the individuals concerned.

Ultimately, we are all one people, united in a common destiny. When we learn to serve each other and to take joy in each other's happiness, we will have performed the greatest mitzvah of all.

"Love is an endless mystery, for it has nothing else to explain it."
Rabindranath Tagore

As we learn to open our hearts wider and wider, so all external considerations begin to fall away.

Eventually, love defines and justifies itself, for it needs no other support and no other references. Love is all-encompassing and, in its purest form, it needs no object on which to alight. It is a state of being, not of doing. It is fed - and it grows - on itself alone. It is not partisan; it takes no sides, it is not judgemental in any way. It simply is.

To cultivate such love takes time and practice and a certain amount of understanding. First, we must be still and look for that quiet centre within ourselves. Then, we must learn to understand and to see that same centre in all other beings. And, lastly, we need to consciously operate and act from that centre, always addressing and appealing to the same place in our fellows.

All of this takes a lifetime of practice. The cultivation of love; the understanding of our essential oneness beyond all external differences: these are the proper goals of human life. To learn to love God, ourselves and our brothers and sisters, and to create a world of peace and justice founded on those principles of love and unity - this is what we are for.

Nothing more is required.

"None of you has faith until he loves for his brother what he loves for himself."
Hadith, Sahih Muslim

The injunction to love others as we love ourselves means that we should wish for all the good things that we desire to be showered upon our brothers and sisters in equal measure.

The world is so bountiful and yet has such limited resources that we must learn to share freely. The very best way to fulfilment and satisfaction is to act as servants to each others' needs and desires. What we would wish for ourselves can be freely given to another, and we can remain secure in the faith that our needs, too, will be seen and met.

Instead of constantly striving to enrich ourselves at the expense of others, think for a moment how different life could be if our greatest wish, our greatest joy, was to be found in acts of service and generosity.

To seek only to serve the self - to create barriers of "yours and mine" is to deny our basic interconnectedness and create a world of selfishness and lack. It is a denial of God's bounty and a negation of faith.

To live in service to others is the surest path to a happier world, to a peaceful heart and, ultimately, to a union with the Divine that such actions evoke and recognise.

"You shall love the Lord your God with all your heart, with all your soul, and with all your might."
Deuteronomy 6:5

To love God with all of our being means - if it means anything - to love all of God's manifestations in the world. To hold love in our hearts for an abstract concept is one thing, attainable, perhaps, through a daily practice of meditation and prayer, but to bring that love to bear on all of God's creation is more challenging. It requires us to learn to look beyond surface differences, to see beyond race, religion, gender, nationality, belief and practice and to find and focus on the God within.

If we believe in God, we must believe in an omnipresent God - one who is literally present in every atom of creation. And if we are to truly love God, then we must be willing to love him in every one of those atoms. We need to tolerate practices we do not share, try to understand what may seem totally incomprehensible to us; to see even our "enemies" as manifestations of God on Earth, and train our hearts, always, in the ways of love.

As we rise above all forms of sectarianism, we begin to approach more closely the realisation that we are all children of one God, all embodiments of His purpose and all part of one great, eternal life.

"But I say to you who hear, Love your enemies, do good to those who hate you."

Luke 6:27

Love takes so many forms and is expressed in so many ways, it is ironic that the greatest trial of love required of us is one that is impersonal and disinterested.

Love in its broadest sense encompasses all people and all things: we are called upon to love all of God's creation, including the things that seem to us ugly or evil or wrong. We are called upon to love even our 'enemies.'

Love that is reciprocated has its own rewards, but love that rises above the personal and takes us into places that are disturbing and difficult: this is the real test of our faith and our resolve. If we wish to live closer to God, in tune with the reality of spiritual life, then we must learn to love and serve all, irrespective of whether we agree with their opinions, lifestyle, politics or choices.

Only by meeting hatred and aggression with a strong and fierce love will we be able to achieve the peace that we all need to live full and happy lives.

If we try to defeat our enemies, we doom ourselves to an endless cycle of violence. If we try to understand them and learn to love them and ourselves in them, we will achieve a lasting peace for all.

"And We have certainly created man, and We know what his soul whispers to him, and We are closer to him than [his] jugular vein."

Quran 50:16

The voices of the world are loud and clamorous. They urge us to identify with this group or that. They urge us to find our fulfilment in material things, to seek after fame, fortune and power; to lose ourselves in physical desire; to crave a fleeting beauty.

But, within each of us, there is a quieter voice waiting to be heard and, when we learn to be still, when we have the courage to close our ears to those distracting cries, we may hear the whisper of our soul that speaks only the truth.

That voice speaks of God's love; of our oneness and interconnection. It tells us that we are all from God and of God and that the soul that whispers in our hearts speaks the same language and says the same thing as the soul in every other child of the dust.

Material life leads to separation: from ourselves, from each other and from God. Spiritual life leads us back to our source: back to a union with our soul's purpose; back to God, back to a life where we are able to be what we were made to be; back to a life of peace and harmony, of knowledge and understanding. Back to the business of manifesting God's love on earth.

"He who loves money will not be satisfied with money, nor he who loves wealth with his income."
Ecclesiastes Rabbah 1:21

What lies at the core of our being is a spiritual reality, a soul, a spark of the Divine: our true, eternal self. When we are disconnected from that self, we feel a dissatisfaction; an unease; a sense of incompleteness; a gap; a void; a hole.

So much in our current world teaches us that the way to fill this void within us is through acquisition of material wealth: more and more money in the bank, smarter, newer cars on the driveway; holiday homes; more clothes, more shoes, more gadgets. If we can only have enough, we will be satisfied.

But the hole within us is not material. It cannot be filled with physical possessions, it has to be filled with things of the spirit: peace, justice, love; the realisation that sharing our resources is more fulfilling than hoarding them; taking down barriers between ourselves feeds us more thoroughly than building walls.

And the process of closing this gap within us starts with a simple daily practice of gratitude and of opening our hearts to each other. It begins in the smile to a stranger; the helping hand to a person in need; in the growing understanding of what it means to believe that we are all expressions and manifestations of one divine life.

"Love is not affectionate feeling but a steady wish for the loved person's ultimate good as far as it can be obtained."

C.S. Lewis

Love takes many forms and appears in many guises, but one thing is constant: it is not selfish or grasping. When we love truly, we care so much for the object of our love that their happiness and well-being become at least as important as our own.

Imagine how it would be if we committed ourselves to learn to love all beings with such a selfless and dispassionate love. Imagine if we stopped our habits of self-protection: in ourselves, our families, our communities, our tribes, religions, our nation-states; even our species!

What if we could rise above our own self-interest and realise that our ultimate well-being is to be found in a world where all people are safe: housed, fed, fulfilled in every way?

The way to a lasting peace in the world is through equity and sharing, justice and fairness for all. And the way to achieve these things is to unclench our grasping hands and open wide our fearful hearts to the possibility and the reality that our need for happiness, security and peace cannot find its fullest expression until these things are a reality for all. It is for this collective fulfilment that we must pray and actively strive.

"Kindness is a mark of faith, and whoever is not kind has no faith."

Hadith, Sahih Muslim

The depth of our understanding of our true selves and of our relationship with God is not to be measured in lofty words but in our actions.

To profess faith in a Divine Being and to enter into a conscious relationship of love with that Being is to acknowledge that the same relationship with the same Being exists for all people, whether they realise it or not. And while we might feel frustration at their inability to see what is clear to us, we have to learn patience, and trust that the love that exists between ourselves and our Creator will find its way into other hearts and, one bright day, into all hearts.

Meanwhile, our faith requires that we are ambassadors of that Divine love, and so our actions and relationships are marked by a disinterested and impersonal love that is distinguished by acts of kindness.

Kindness is one of the most attractive characteristics that a person can manifest in their dealings with others, because it acknowledges a commonality of experience and the possibility of connection on a level that is selfless and true. To believe in an omnipresent God is to strive to see the Divine in everything. And, seeing it, of course we must be kind.

"Do not seek revenge or bear a grudge against anyone among your people, but love your neighbour as yourself. I am the Lord."

Leviticus 19:18

We have all done things of which we are not proud. If we wish to live happy, balanced lives in which we can feel and express all the positive emotions that a human being can feel, we have to learn to forgive ourselves and move on, shaken but unbowed; determined to do better.

And once we have uncovered the capacity for self-forgiveness, we need to turn it outwards, into the world, and apply it to others. We will not always be able to understand another's actions, but we can learn patience, tolerance and kindness. We can learn forbearance and, through that, forgiveness.

Just as we become emotionally stunted if we cannot forgive ourselves, so our relations in the outer world – with family, friends and strangers – can become twisted and cruel if we do not learn to forgive and forbear. Our default position needs to be one of openness and benevolent curiosity rather than a clenched, closed-in fear.

Forgiveness bestows freedom to all parties, on all sides of the action or behaviour in question. It is often difficult; sometimes it seems impossible in the face of terrible violence and worse, but, still, it is the only road that leads, by way of justice, to peace.

"And lower to them the wing of humility out of mercy and say, 'My Lord, have mercy upon them as they brought me up [when I was] small.'"

Quran 17:24

As human beings, our wants and needs are few and well-defined. We need love and security to thrive emotionally; food and a safe roof over our heads; freedom from fear and oppression; freedom to express and be ourselves; peace; justice; a life that shares the bounties of our beautiful world.

We all try our best to achieve these things for ourselves and our connections and, in any given moment, we make decisions and choices that we hope will lead us to these desired outcomes.

But not all of them do! We are fallible creatures and we make mistakes. As individuals, we often put ourselves first, not understanding that it is in the collective good that we will find all the things we need. As nation states or religious groups, we identify too narrowly and look to the interests of 'us' over and above the interests of 'them.' Again, we fail to realise that the well-being of all depends on the well-being of all. None of us, individuals or groups, can live in a vacuum. We are all interdependent and must learn to find our fulfilment through helping others to find theirs.

The mercy and forgiveness that we look for must first take root in our own hearts.

"Love unaccompanied by criticism is not love."
Talmud, Arachin 16b

The love that we are called upon to cultivate as we move closer to God is one that is impersonal and unconditional. It is a love born out of true connection.

At the same time, we find ourselves in particular physical relationships with our fellow creatures. In other words, for whatever reason, we are born into particular families within particular communities. We make friends along our way and have encounters with people from whom we may learn and whom we might teach, albeit unconsciously.

The love that we cultivate for particular connections is different from the impersonal love we carry for strangers. It contains a level of inter-personal responsibility. These are our close fellow-travellers on our road back to God and we must believe that they serve a purpose and a function in our lives, as we do in theirs.

This responsibility means that we must both be willing to accept criticism and willing to offer it wherever it seems appropriate. This, too, is an expression of love: it demonstrates care, and it is another way in which we can manifest our understanding of inter-connectedness. It lets us teach and learn the lessons we most need at this time and in this place in order to become our true selves.

"Love is the only force capable of transforming an enemy into a friend."

Martin Luther King Jr.

To consider another as our enemy is to deny their eternal connection with us. It is to deny the unity of life, and even the existence and benevolence of the Supreme Being from which that one life springs.

To see enemies where there are only fellow humans means that we are attached to false identifications with nation, religion, race, ideology, tribe or whatever. It means that we have chosen to live in a world of disconnection and individuality rather than the true world of connection and oneness.

Love lies at the core of our being and once we learn to accept that fact, it becomes impossible to see our fellow creatures as separate or different from ourselves. We are all sprung from the same stock, all sharers in the trials and travails of this human existence. The things we have in common far outweigh our material differences, and the better we come to understand our true nature, the more clearly we will see our true relationship with each other.

We are all embodiments of the Divine. Every one of us is here to manifest and represent the Godhead here on earth. Every one of us carries within our mortal frame the spirit, the very essence of love. There are no enemies here.

"The Lord your God is in your midst, a mighty one who will save; he will rejoice over you with gladness; he will quiet you by his love."
Zephaniah 3:17

We can interpret such a claim to mean that God is present and with us collectively in our synagogues, churches or mosques. Wherever we are gathered in His name, He is there.

But what if it means something else as well? That God is, literally, in the centre – the midst – of each one of us individually too? That within our hearts we carry a spark of the divine life and that, if we let it speak to us, it offers us salvation from our suffering and our doubt; it offers us gladness, joy, and true peace of the spirit?

And if God lives in every heart, how can we fight and make war on each other? How can we deny basic comforts to each other? How can we be content to allow suffering of any kind when we know that the person suffering is also an embodiment of the same God who actuates us?

In truth it is impossible to be God-conscious and indifferent to our fellows. Every one that lives is part of us on the deepest level; we are brothers, sisters, parents and children to each other. We have responsibilities, a moral duty, to search within ourselves for what is divine and then learn to see it in others.

"Love is patient, love is kind. It does not envy, it does not boast, it is not proud."

1 Corinthians 13:4

True love, founded on spiritual values, is an endlessly open heart. It is the very essence of patience because it forgives all transgressions, time and again. It waits for the truth to dawn in another's heart, without judgement and without fear.

Love is kindness, too, because kindness and patience are intertwined: they each need the other to grow and blossom.

But true love is not blind. While earthly love may close its eyes to faults and imperfections in the beloved, spiritual love sees clearly. It watches from a perspective of eternity and it understands that truth will dawn in every heart when the right circumstances arise.

Two builders are cutting stone to fit. One strikes his stone once and it splits. We watch the other strike the stone twenty times to achieve the same result. What is different? Only that we were not there to see the first nineteen strikes of the first builder.

So it is with this love that we are learning to feel and share with the world. Trust is necessary; patience is necessary; faith is necessary. Our love, our kindness, our patience will see the things we dream of come to pass if we can only remember what we are and where we come from.

"And those who believe and do righteous deeds are the companions of Paradise; they will abide therein eternally."

Quran 2:82

There is a particular quality, or tone to truth that resonates within us when we live in alignment with what we truly are. There is no guilt, no shadow of a "should have."

In these moments of alignment with our purpose, we are undoubtedly 'companions of Paradise' because the spirit of the Divine fills us and walks with us. The troubles of the world recede and truth steps forward, carrying with it the quiet joy of the promise of perfection.

How fiercely we ought to pursue these moments! How wonderful it would be to extend these heavenly insights so that all of our days are filled with the scents and miasmas of a greater reality!

Through our faith and its resulting deeds of kindness and service, each one of us could live in the sure understanding that perfection is possible. It is within our grasp, a flicker, a hair's breadth away.

If I live in such a way that I feel the breath of Paradise on me and if you do the same, will we not be in Paradise together? Will this whole world not feel what it is to be in Paradise? And, having tasted such perfection, will we not make it our life's work to maintain it?

"In a place where there is no humanity, strive to be human."

Pirkei Avot 2:6

It is so easy for us to be knocked off course by daily events. Even something as minor as a careless word in the street or an accidental shove in a crowd can cause anger to rise within us. When we are faced with purposeful and sustained aggression or hatred, how can we maintain our equilibrium?

To be fully human is to be open and connected. It is to see and feel and care. It is to understand that we are all part of one great life. So when violence and war and other horrors separate us into factions, how can we retain our humanity? How can we continue to see the truth of our oneness?

A daily practice is necessary, for one thing. Unless we train ourselves in positive habits of thought, our mind, like an atrophied muscle, will lack the strength it needs to hold firm in adversity. Faith is needed: our unshakeable belief that our true nature is to be found in love and unity, and not in hatred and separation. We will need courage, too, to speak up for what we know is right; and firmness of purpose: we cannot speak and leave. We must stay the course. We must keep speaking out against injustice and not rest until it is rooted out.

Train yourself to look at your 'enemy' and see God incarnate. Take a deep breath. Stay human.

"The first duty of love is to listen."
Paul Tillich

Love grows out of compassion and empathy. It sees and feels; it is understanding, sensitive and kind.

But love is also strong. Sweet words are always pleasing, but love can withstand truth in all its guises, even when it is unpalatable and hard to hear. If the first duty of love is to listen, then a parallel duty is for it to speak truthfully and openly.

Division grows between people when they do not understand each other. Resentments grow. fear grows. We withdraw into the familiar and safe, leaving the rest outside the scope of our sympathies.

But to speak clearly and openly – and to know that you have been heard: this is a sure formula for peace. This is fertile ground for the seeds of love to grow.

To listen well, with focus; to hear, understand and assimilate what you are hearing: this is a great gift, a great blessing – a great bestower of peace.

If I tell you what troubles me and you feel it as keenly as I do; if I hear your woes and feel your pain, will that not bring us closer together? Will we not understand each other more deeply?

In speaking truthfully to each other, and in listening with open hearts, we will surely find a way to peace.

"Do not be people without minds of your own, saying that if others treat you well, you will treat them well, and that if they do wrong, you will do wrong. Instead, accustom yourselves to do good if people do good and not to do wrong if they do evil."

Hadith, Al-Tirmidhi

To be fully at peace ourselves and to be vehicles by which God's peace may enter the world, we need a firm resolve to be and do our best at all times.

It is good to be able to adapt ourselves to different circumstances and to allow for the differences in customs and behaviour that we will undoubtedly encounter in our dealings with others, but we also need to stay true to ourselves.

The bedrock of our faith is simple: we are all God's creatures; all sharers of one life and one destiny. Anything that serves to increase our sense of unity is good. Whatever creates division and strife between us must be challenged, questioned and addressed.

So when we see others act in such a way that creates distance, fear or hatred between people, we must hold firm to our understanding that this is wrong. We must not join in, but should look, whenever we can, for ways in which we might bring the healing balm of love, peace and justice to bear. If we are to be worthy ambassadors of the Divine, we must be prepared to act on what we know to be true.

"Hatred stirs up strife, but love covers all offences."
Proverbs 10:12

We human beings are the inheritors of such greatness: we are the place where Divine nature and materiality meet and intertwine. At our best, we are able to manifest the very spirit and essence of the Godhead; and at our worst, we are worse than animals, capable of such atrocities that are hard to contemplate and impossible to speak of.

Each of us carries this dual nature within our heart, and it is up to us which one will predominate in our lives. Our animal nature, if not tamed and animated by our spiritual, will lead us to hatred, division and strife. Ruled by the ego, we see only the illusion of difference.

But, once we learn to see with eyes that are attuned to spiritual reality, we understand that there is no deep difference between us. Beyond the temporary physical illusions of colour, race, creed, nation, religion and so on, there is an eternal truth of oneness that leads us on to the path of love.

And where love reigns, there can be no offences between us. Where love reigns, there can only be kindness, patience, understanding, forbearance and forgiveness. Where love reigns, there is unity, togetherness and peace. Where love reigns, God is present and we do His work.

"And over all these virtues put on love, which binds them all together in perfect unity."

Colossians 3:14

Love is not the only virtue. We are capable of doing good in many ways and on many levels. Honesty, courage, kindness, compassion; generosity, integrity, fairness; temperance in all things, fortitude of spirit, prudence, justice: all of these are virtues to live by. They give us a framework by which we can lead lives of value and worth. By upholding them, we will add to the peace and prosperity of ourselves, our families, our communities and the world at large.

But all virtues have a corresponding vice, and without some means to regulate ourselves, doing good can quickly turn from being an act of service to a justification for selfishness and vanity.

And – of course – it is love that will set us on the right way. Not love of self, nor love of praise, but a love based on principles that are strong and true: a love based on a correct understanding of who and what we are in ourselves; and on who and what we are in relation to each other and to God.

Think of it like this: all our virtues are like the clothes we put on to go out into the world to go about our business. Love is the final layer: a warm and weatherproof cloak that protects us from the elements and keeps us dry and safe.

"And the servants of the Most Merciful are those who walk upon the earth in humility."

Quran 25:63

It is impossible for us to fully comprehend the path that another walks in life. We cannot know what inner battles he or she must fight; we cannot anticipate the lessons he or she still needs to learn to be free of the illusion of difference.

But we can still connect with them because we are able, always, to speak and appeal to the Divine spark that lies at the core of each of us. We can trust that that spark will be uncovered in each of us in the fullness of time. We just need to understand that we are all at a different point on the path that leads us all to the Godhead.

We look up to those ahead of us on that path and seek their wisdom and guidance; we, in turn, help those who walk behind. And, sometimes, it is given to us to walk in joy alongside those whose level of understanding is close to our own.

But the point is this: we are not gods who know all things. It is hard enough to know ourselves, and with so much unknown, it would be an arrogance in us to dictate how another should live or what another should believe. That is God's work and, whilst we may encourage and model the understanding we hope will dawn, we should trust that He will do it – and in His own time.

"The reward of a mitzvah (good deed) is the mitzvah itself."

Talmud, Pirkei Avot 4:2

Perhaps the worst feeling that we can experience at moments of change in the world is one of helplessness or powerlessness. We live in a time when we are able to witness every disaster, every crisis, every atrocity in the world. We see so much wrong, so much suffering, that we can feel overwhelmed and paralysed by it.

And what can we do? We might raise money for the causes we believe in, or go on marches to make a stand for what we believe is right, We protest and sign petitions. We make a noise. But, even so, we can end up feeling that these things are little more than gestures.

On an individual level, within our families, our social groups and our local communities, there is much that we can do to maintain a level of peace and harmony. On this smaller scale, each one of us can make a real difference and, when we do – if we all do it – we will influence and affect the greater picture too.

How joyful it is, then, when we are in a position to do some meaningful good. Every small act of kindness or consideration or compassion adds to the well-being of all of us. To have the opportunity to help in any way is, undoubtedly, a great gift.

*"Come forth into the light of things,
Let nature be your teacher."*
William Wordsworth

Sit for a moment. Close your eyes and imagine you are in a wood or forest. The sun is shining and all the life around you is stretching upwards to light and warmth. Every tree, every flower, every plant is yearning and rising towards the light.

Now look deep within yourself. Imagine your heart, your soul, your true self, longing and reaching out for spiritual light in the same way that the trees and flowers grow towards the sun. Feel your whole inner being lift; feel how, in your heart, you long to merge with the light that shines down from above. Let yourself be bathed in the light for a time. Let it fill you with its peace. Do nothing for a moment. Think nothing. Be there, in the light.

This is our work as human beings: to make ourselves one with the great light that is wisdom, strength and beauty; that is knowledge and understanding; that is peace and justice and unfailing love, pure and true. It is there for us at all times, waiting for us to reach out to it.

Like the trees, the flowers and the plants, let us strive – without striving – to make our lives a natural merging into light.

"Love is the beauty of the soul."
Saint Augustine

True love is, without doubt, the crowning glory of human attainment. It is not just an emotion or a feeling, subject to the whims of mood and circumstance. Neither is it a gift to be bestowed upon one special person only. It is not something limited to family or nation, to religion or race.

True love is a state of being, achieved through practice, that keeps us held in a correct relationship with each other and with the whole of creation. True love flows through us and from us, in proportion to our ability to remove the blockages that impede it. Egotism, self-interest, greed, avarice, envy: everything that creates barriers between us serves to strengthen the dam that prevents the flow of love.

If we are to be vehicles through which God's love enters the world; if we are to allow our true nature to direct our actions; if we are to experience and attain this state of love, then we must work towards it with all our being. Meditation and moments of deep introspection help us uncover our true selves and root out the darkness and trauma we all carry. Prayer aligns us with the Higher Power that offers us love unconditionally, and acts of kindness, generosity and service open our hearts to the possibility and the beauty of love flowing between us without impediment.

"When a person's faith is not strong unless he gives up arguing, he has no faith."

Hadith, Abu Dawood

It's impossible to 'argue' someone into having faith and it's foolish to try. A believer needs no proof of God's existence, but however strong their faith, they can neither persuade nor empirically prove God's existence to a person who is not ready to embrace the possibility of a higher power.

And that's okay. It is not our task to prove God's existence, nor to force others to believe. If our faith is true, we can be sure that all things proceed as they should. All things will come to pass in their allotted time. We can allow God to work in His own way.

But this does not mean that we must remain silent. We can show by our faith that, through it, there awaits the possibility of a fuller and more joyful life. Through our understanding of our relationship to our Originator, through our fanning of the Divine spark we have found within our hearts, we illuminate the truth of Brotherhood, Sisterhood – Oneness – with all humankind.

If we wish to persuade others that a God-centred life is the best life to live, and if we wish to demonstrate the essential unity of all life, then we must demonstrate our understanding by living in kindness, harmony and love. That is the strongest argument of all.

"Nation shall not lift up sword against nation, neither shall they learn war any more."

Isaiah 2:4

It seems that warfare is hard-wired into the human psyche. The history of the western world is a litany of war, appropriation and oppression. Christianity was spread through conquest; Islam too. Even the original Israelite settlement of the land of Canaan was through violence and the displacement of others.

Looked at from a humanitarian point of view, war is clearly a manifestation of some kind of madness or psychological illness: no other species kills its own kind in the way that we do. All wars are a failure of diplomacy, and represent the defeat of humanity by bestiality. The idea that we can solve our differences through violence is, in itself, mad.

And as for these 'differences.' What are they? They centre around identity, be it national, religious, tribal or cultural. They centre around land and the ownership of land. They centre around resources and the exploitation of those resources. They centre, always, around materiality and a false identification with the body.

When we learn to see ourselves as primarily spiritual beings, living on a planet that has everything we need for us all to survive and thrive: then our swords may indeed become ploughshares.

"And if thou draw out thy soul to the hungry, and satisfy the afflicted soul; then shall thy light rise in obscurity, and thy darkness be as the noonday:"

Isaiah 58:10

When we are trammelled up in self-care and self-centredness, it is difficult for us to let our light shine as it should. Sometimes we are so preoccupied with our own progress along the path, so taken up with our own study and learning, that we forget the one thing that brings us into the fullness of our being: service.

As soon as we act for the welfare of others rather than ourselves; as soon as we consider another's needs above our own, even for a moment, we move out of the self-centre and into a liminal space where we become more than just ourselves: we become merged with something higher; something that unites us with all life; something that recognises, lives and exists in a state of true brotherhood.

Our own well-being is vitally important, as is our own study, contemplation and growth in understanding. But all of these things count for nothing until they are tempered, strengthened and brightened in the fire of selfless service to others. We cannot comprehend true brotherhood, nor will we find lasting peace until we are truly brothers and sisters to all.

"And the servants of the Most Merciful are those who, when they are addressed, say words of peace."
Quran 25:63

An evolved being is one who is at peace within him- or her-self. They have no desire to impose their beliefs or their way of living on others; they understand the nature of the path that we all walk, and they see the need for each individual soul to achieve its own enlightenment in its own time.

An evolved being speaks words of peace because they know we are of one nature and from one source, and that our natural state is one of perfect harmony.

All bodily identification is an illusion, a temporary state, and, whilst it is good to contemplate the lessons that might be learned by being in a particular body at a particular time, the greatest lesson we can learn is that we are not our bodies. Comprehending this great truth frees us from all the material attachments that lead to conflict and war. This is the great truth that opens up the possibility of a world that is just, loving and peaceful.

An evolved being speaks words of peace because they know that they are speaking to themselves and to God, who are both ever-present in the heart of the 'other.'

But an evolved being is not special or different. They are us, a little further along the path. Let us strive to follow them.

"Peace I leave with you; my peace I give you. I do not give to you as the world gives. Do not let your hearts be troubled and do not be afraid."

John 14:27

Peace is not a state that is imposed from outside. Peace between neighbours, communities, tribes and nations arises naturally out of a peace that is attained internally.

All of us carry within our heart a spark of the Divine. Each of us has the capability to centre ourselves in that spark and to be actuated by a deep understanding of our true place and role in this fleeting earthly life.

We are beings of light, eternally interwoven in the oneness of all things. Our bodies are made of ancient stardust; we carry the imprint of every stage of our evolution, from gross matter to pure spirit. Our task is to manifest this knowledge; to be a conscious part of the material universe coming to know itself.

Knowing the truth of what we are and what we are for is the first step to peace and a just and loving world. If we find the truth of ourselves, we will find the truth of all, and then there can be no more war; no more 'us and them;' there can be only 'us.'

Be still and look within your heart. Ask for the truth to be revealed to you. Listen for the answer. Trust it. Your peace and safety are God-given.

Yet have I set my king upon my holy hill of Zion.
I will declare the decree: the LORD hath said unto me,
Thou art my Son; this day have I begotten thee.

Psalm 2

When we first set our feet on the spiritual path, we can find ourselves in a lonely place. In many cases we are creating a divide, not only between ourselves and the everyday world, but we are also drawing a line in our own lives between what has gone before and what will come after. We have reached a point where we are ready to take responsibility for our own development as human beings – moral and spiritual – and reject the materialistic consumerism that threatens to destroy us all.

When we chart a course against the prevailing winds of the world, we encounter rough seas and many storms. Anger, hatred, mistrust: these have plagued seekers and mystics throughout the ages and on many levels, both visible and invisible and they may raise their ugly heads to plague us even now.

But let us not worry. We know that a world of open-hearted support lies before us. The promise of peace becomes stronger and more real with every step we take, and we know, deep down, that our strength is founded on something lasting and infinitely reliable.

"Let your light so shine before men, that they may see your good works, and glorify your Father which is in heaven."
Matthew 5:16

When we allow ourselves to become vehicles through which light may come into the world; when we learn to clear our hearts of vain and unbecoming thoughts; when we free ourselves from sectarian allegiances, we begin to align ourselves with our true nature and our true purpose.

None of us is God, of course, but every one of us carries within our hearts a spark of the Divine, and our great task in life is to uncover that spark, to let it shine out from us as individuals so that our lives become an unpolluted expression of light and truth. To manifest God's light on earth is our primary purpose and through living in such a way as to manifest Godly qualities, we aim, ultimately, for such perfection.

Our human selves are vital and beautiful vehicles for the spirit we carry. and we should care for ourselves and for others with love and appreciation. But we should not forget the higher life that dwells within. Every opening of our hearts and minds that we achieve through acts of service and compassion allows a little more light into the world.

"Great is peace, as even God's name is suspended for the sake of peace."

Talmud, Gittin 59b

Nothing should prevent us from offering aid and succour to those in need. The deepest meditation or the most profound and heartfelt prayer mean nothing if they are done while others around us are suffering.

Everyone is a living embodiment of the Divine and, as such, everyone represents and manifests God on Earth. Whilst it is good to understand that all suffering is as illusory as the body and senses that experience it, it remains our duty to demonstrate our unity by doing all that we can to relieve the suffering of others.

Whilst there are people in the world who are sick from curable diseases, hungry from manufactured lack, dying from avoidable war, none of us can truly be at peace because all suffering, sickness, hunger and violence touch us and prevent us doing what we are here to do. We cannot be God's ambassadors unless we are willing to do His work.

And what is God's work? To love and serve each other; to hold each other up; to help each other along the path that leads from darkness to light.

Peace, internal and external; peace, local and global: this is our aim and our task. It is a great task and a daunting one but it has the highest sanction. We will have the help we need if we only ask.

"The Lord bless you and keep you; the Lord make his face to shine upon you and be gracious to you; the Lord lift up his countenance upon you and give you peace."
Numbers 6:24-26

God's blessings and love are offered to us unconditionally. We do not need to act in particular ways to be worthy of it, we became worthy when He breathed His life into us.

However, if we want to fully embody the love that is offered to us, we must be prepared to live our lives in a way that does not impede the free-flowing of grace. Erecting barriers between people is a sure way to create a block between ourselves and our spiritual birthright, whilst promoting love and harmony is a sure way to help it flow freely.

In other words, whilst God's love is offered without condition, it is up to us to open ourselves to receive it. By freeing our thoughts from restrictive dogma and opening our hearts wide to receive all of humankind as our brothers and sisters, we become clear channels for the life of the universe to work through us.

We are beings of light and love, even if we are currently confined in limited physical frames. Our natural state is one of harmony and peace. With daily effort, and a willingness to search deep within our hearts, we will find out what we truly are.

"Don't turn away. Keep your gaze on the bandaged place. That's where the light enters you."

Rumi

There is a real, and understandable, desire in us to avoid pain, both physical and emotional. It is part of our natural survival instinct and it keeps us from excessive harm. It is, undoubtedly, an instinct to be followed and cultivated.

And yet, it is also true that pain – emotional and physical – brings us great opportunities for learning. When the body is hurt or begins to deteriorate with age or illness, the light of spirit may shine out more strongly. When our emotions are damaged through unkindness or more serious trauma, we are given the possibility to rise above them and find a place of calm – a steady centre – from which to be observers.

It is right and proper to avoid pain and suffering where we can, and to alleviate the suffering of others if it is within our power to do so. But pain and suffering are our travelling companions in this material world, so when we encounter them, we must learn to embrace them; to accept the teachings that they bring us, and to move through them to a place of peace.

"But I say to you that everyone who is angry with his brother will be liable to judgment; whoever insults his brother will be liable to the council; and whoever says, 'You fool!' will be liable to hell of fire."

Matthew 5:22

Anger and hatred directed at another person or group of people always lead to bad feeling. However justified we may feel, whatever the provocation, anger rising up within us is like an uncontrollable flood that is unable to distinguish between the rational and the irrational. It sweeps away everything in its path, the good and the bad.

We are endowed with reason as well as feelings. We have the capacity to think and discuss. Every time anger carries us away in its self-righteous grip, we surrender everything that makes us 'civilised' and become creatures beyond reason or rationality.

This holds true between individuals as well as groups, even nations. When anger overwhelms us, we are a danger to ourselves and to others. We risk imposing inhuman solutions (which solve nothing) onto human problems. Anger neither supports nor calms.

If we are to avoid the hell that anger can lead us into, we must prepare ourselves in advance to resist it. We must try to stay calm and, in the long term, undertake to train our minds to be ruled by rational thought instead of irrational waves of emotion.

"Allah calls to the Home of Peace and guides whom He wills to a straight path."

Quran 10:25

A quiet mind and a heart at peace are our birthright, but material life lays down a film of dust on the shining mirror of our soul. That layer of dirt is followed by another, and then another, until the beauty and simplicity of our true selves is overlaid with the trauma and difficulties of our daily lives.

School and work and the daily grind; political unrest; environmental destruction; climate upheaval; war; conflict; epidemics: all of these things serve to cloud and obscure the clarity and luminescence of our souls. They deaden and cover the divine spark within us, until we forget our selves and our source.

But, whilst it may be covered, it is not extinguished. The light of God shines eternally in all our hearts and the process by which we may be able to wash away the dust of material life is available to us at any time, in any and every moment.

We need to live in truth, in a relationship of love and care for our fellows; to look within our hearts to find the light that shines there; to be still and silent and to listen for the voice that speaks. All that we need to find peace lies within our hearts. God is there too and His voice calls us to stop our struggling, to rest, to know that we are home.

"So God created mankind in his own image, in the image of God he created them;"

Genesis 1:27

We are more than the physical body that we currently inhabit. We carry the imprint of Divinity within these mortal frames and, whilst the physical part of us may be earthbound and temporary, there lies, at our core, a spark of the Divine life that is eternal and unchanging.

If we lift a burning ember out of the fire, we can see that it has all the attributes of the fire, but it is not the fire itself. If we were to lift a teaspoon of water from the ocean, we can understand that it would have all the properties of the ocean, but it is not the ocean.

So it is with this divine spark within us. It is from God and of God, but, of course, it is not God.

If we are to live in a world of peace and harmony, where justice and love prevail, we must find a way to lessen identification with our physical selves and connect with the part that is spiritual and eternal and which, it follows, is the same in each of us.

Equity, justice, peace and love on a material level are noble aspirations for which all good people strive. On the spiritual plane, they are simple facts and the more we bring spiritual consciousness to our lives, the more beautiful our lives will become.

"If you want to make peace, you don't talk to your friends. You talk to your enemies."

Desmond Tutu

We are naturally drawn to people who share similar experiences and values to us. Our societies are structured so that we are all born with particular attachments and identities ready formed. A Ghanaian Christian; a Moroccan Jew; an English Moslem; a Native American. Whatever combination of identities we are born into or choose to adopt as we grow, we see the world through filters that reflect the experiences of those groups.

As a result, we live amongst people who reinforce our own world view and when we ask, "Is this how it is?" We mostly get a "Yes" because we are asking the people who see things like we do.

This is all fine, but, in fact, if we wish to gain a wider understanding of the world, we will need to go beyond our own community and learn to look with a different set of eyes and to feel the results of a different set of experiences.

Talking to our own is reassuring and comforting and is something we rightly seek out. But it it does not add to the wider understandings we need to create a world of peace and justice. The 'bubbles' we all live in provide a measure of comfort, but when conflict rages, we do not need to make peace with our friends.

"Depart from evil, and do good; seek peace and pursue it."

Psalms 34:14

The peace that we seek within our own hearts and in the world at large does not exist piecemeal, but is a network of interwoven strands. Like the hidden roots of trees, or like the mycelium of fungi that pass nourishment along invisible strands, so peace spreads and grows between us in relation to the number of us who seek it out.

To sit quietly and to quieten the mind; to pray for and meditate upon peace; to feel it for a moment and to carry it with us as we go about our daily lives – these things are acts of service to the greater good of humanity and are practical ways in which we can make the world a better and saner place for all.

But, in a world riven by conflict and separation, we must also manifest peace, not just in our own hearts, but also in the outer world. We must promote peace in all our interactions; we must call for peace in all our protests; demand it from our leaders; speak out against violence in all of its forms.

And if we are firm in our resolve, our determination to achieve peace will help to create a fair and just world in which peace can thrive. Peace, like justice, is a political outcome and neither can exist without the other.

"Blessed are the peacemakers, for they will be called children of God."
Matthew 5:9

If we believe in a Supreme Being then it follows that we would want to live in such a way as will bring us into closer alignment with Him. It is why we look always to adopt values that enhance the spiritual and focus less on the outer illusions to which we are all subject.

Sometimes we frame it as seeking God's approval, but it is really about the naturally good feeling that flows through us when we live according to the Divine principles of universal love and unity. It is not so much a question of winning God's approval, for we always have that, irrespective of how we live; it is about the state of grace that arises naturally when we are in tune with our source.

The great path to our own salvation and enlightenment, and the way in which we may hasten the salvation and enlightenment of others, may be followed simply in the constant promotion of love, peace and justice between all people.

We can feel when we are in tune with our highest selves and the feeling is a good one: not smug, not self-righteous – just good and positive. Living in this state of attunement opens the doors of Divine energy into our hearts and that is a blessing indeed.

*"Light is more important than the lantern,
The poem more important than the notebook."*
Nizar Qabbani

On the one hand, it is important to recognise that, whilst we cannot, for example, carry water without a bucket, ultimately it is not the bucket that is important, but the water it contains.

The vehicle by which knowledge comes to us is not as important as the knowledge itself, although the vehicle is both necessary and valuable.

So it is with all the virtues to which we aspire. So it is with the world we wish to create. Peace, love, justice: these are the important things. These represent the water in our bucket. The bucket itself is anything that can deliver these things, religion or politics; top-down or grass-roots, it doesn't matter. What matters is the result: that the balm of peace reaches those who suffer; that food reaches the hungry; that shelter reaches the homeless; that medicines reach the sick.

None of these things is beyond the power of humankind to achieve. What is lacking, at the moment, is the will to see it done.

Light is light, whatever the lamp. There may be differences in our beliefs, but some things we know are eternally true: that we are the creatures of one Divine source; brothers and sisters; outward expressions of the one Divine life.

"The exceeding brightness of this early sun
Makes me conceive how dark I have become."
Wallace Stevens

We look upon the light as something to aspire to: we yearn for it and work so hard to attain it. And yet, when we find it, we come to learn that it is not necessarily kind. In fact, the light we seek can, at first, appear harsh and terrifying because it illuminates our life without any filter, and it allows us no place to hide. We are completely exposed for what we are: all our actions – good and bad, positive and negative, honourable and otherwise – can be seen. All of our hidden motives – sometimes even hidden from ourselves – are there for us to see in all their nakedness.

But the light is not unkind either. It does not judge us or punish us: the voice of our own conscience is punishment enough. If we have the courage to face what the light reveals to us; if we can accept ourselves for what we are and what we have been; if we can forgive ourselves for all that we have done and failed to do: then all is burned away and turned to ashes in the light, as offerings in a sacrificial flame.

And so the light proves to be neither kind nor unkind, but something greater than both: total acceptance, full expiation and unreserved love. And what the light offers to us, we can share with others.

"A man who refuses light will remain in the darkness even by the side of light!"
Mehmet Murat ildan

Whilst it is true that light is our birthright and the very substance of our being, it is equally true that, in this material world, we must dig in the rubble of our lives, and excavate our very foundations, if we are to find what lies buried within these corporeal frames.

A room cannot be flooded with light until we open the curtains; we cannot see the dawn until we open our eyes; we cannot find our way until we begin to look where we are going.

So it is with spiritual light: it is there for us, always, but we must do what needs to be done to allow it to shine on and in and through us. We must learn to draw back the veils of ignorance that lie before us; we must learn to open our eyes to the truth that surrounds us in every waking moment; and, through study and contemplation, we must learn to see the path that stretches from our feet to the distant hills from where the light comes.

With open eyes, we see what is there to be seen. With eyes tight shut, all is darkness. Our task is to learn to open our eyes and accept the truth that thus lies open before us: all is one; all is light; all is love.

*"A tree forms itself in answer
to its place and the light.
Explain it how you will, the only
thing explainable will be
your explanation."*

Wendell Berry

We are all the product of our environment: the places and events of our childhoods; the love or otherwise of parents and guardians; siblings; school – everything that we see and hear and experience goes into making us who we are at any given moment in our lives. These things, perhaps more than we fully realise, are the building blocks of our present personalities and they determine our response to trauma; our interactions with others; our levels of happiness; even our predisposition to faith.

And yet, an oak that has grown twisted and stunted by rock and wind is still in essence an oak. It still has the bark, the leaves, the nature of an oak. It still drops acorns to the floor.

So are we, however formed by our childhoods, still essentially human; we still have the capacity for love; we still carry within our hearts that divine spark that is not touched or troubled by worldly calamity and misfortune.

This is the true centre of our being. Our primary task is to find it and live in its light.

"The strong person is not the good wrestler. Rather, the strong person is the one who controls himself when he is angry."

Hadith, Sahih al-Bukhari

The quality of the body is not necessarily relevant to the success of a particular life. Of course, a healthy body is a great gift and it allows us the opportunity to experience the world in its fullness, but to spend too much time on bodily matters is to create an imbalance and risk missing what is truly important.

Our bodies are the instruments by which we learn the lessons of this earthly school. They carry us through the intricacies of family and nation, of religion, creed, colour and gender. They allow us to explore and to play and appreciate the wonders and the beauty of the universe in which we live.

But even the strongest body will age. The hardest muscles will grow slack, the firmest, smoothest skin will sag and wrinkle. The important lessons are not carried in muscle and skin and bone; they exist on a finer plane, in self-control and self-knowledge.

If we live life in the mistaken opinion that we are physical beings only, we will be overcome when our bodies fail us. If we practice living in the knowledge of our spiritual reality, when the time comes, we will be held in safety, and death will hold no terrors for us.

"Peace is not merely a distant goal but the journey itself."
St. Teresa of Calcutta

Peace is always attainable, but it is more than just the absence of violence. We can, and must, call for a ceasefire and an end to hostilities, but that does necessarily mean that we are at peace, only that our violence or anger is contained.

The desire for peace, the willingness to work for it and the understanding of the need for it are the preconditions needed to achieve it. It is not about conceding this or that piece of land, or this or that resource. Peace is there, always, as a natural state of being within our hearts.

If we can just stop for a moment to be still and breathe calmly, we can look within and find the peace that rests there. We can feel the joy of it, the rightness, the way it envelops and uplifts us; the way it seeks to spread out from us into the world.

Peace is not something we move towards; not something we can attain through effort; it is with us, here and now, our constant companion on our journey through life. We can choose to ignore it but, if we embrace it, we give ourselves the greatest of gifts: freedom from fear. And that enables us to share the gift with the world: peace unbounded; peace universal; peace that stays with us, wherever we go.

"Great peace have those who love your law; nothing can make them stumble."

Psalms 119:165

We all need a safe passage through the trials of this world. No life is free of difficulties, and the certainties of old-age, illness and death come to all in the end: rich or poor, high or low.

To sail through the storms of life requires a boat that will hold us steady when winds blow and waves threaten to engulf us.

Some think that material wealth will protect them and, for a while at least, it might appear to do so. But death is no respecter of gold or silver; you can drive a Bugatti or you can walk on dusty bare feet: death will come.

So how can we prepare ourselves for what life will undoubtedly throw at us? If material wealth is no defence against supra-physical events, what is?

To be conscious of, and centred in, our true selves is to be anchored firmly in a calm bay where even the strongest storm cannot touch us, where the ravages of time and mortality cannot shake us. It is something that needs practice, however: a routine of discipline and introspection that will teach us patience and fortitude.

If safety lies in God's law, it is up to us to find and follow that law, which we can do through self-knowledge, service and love.

"And the peace of God, which transcends all understanding, will guard your hearts and your minds..."

Philippians 4:7

When we talk about the peace of God and how it "transcends all understanding," we can fall into the mistake of thinking that it is difficult to comprehend and is, therefore almost impossible to attain.

It might be better to reframe "transcends all understanding" to be closer in meaning to "transcends all efforts to define it." because the peace of God is not difficult to apprehend, even if we lack the words that help us comprehend it.

Like so much in life, God's peace does not reveal its treasures to the intellect. The truth, here, is more kinetic – it must be lived and experienced to be fully appreciated.

Perhaps we cannot define God's peace, but we can all experience it by learning to sit quietly for a few moments during our fraught and busy days. A few deep breaths; a gradual quietening of the mind: and it is there, waiting for us to enter into it: a gift given freely and without stint.

It is this lived experience of inner peace that will set right our relationships, that will allay our fears and soothe our troubled hearts. It is this that will protect and guard us.

"Great is peace, for the name of God is peace."
Midrash Tanhuma, Pekudei 3

The positive accomplishments of the human race are breathtaking in their scope and beauty. Think for a moment of the great works of art and architecture that we have built to soar over us and lift our minds heavenwards: the great temples and mosques; the ancient cathedrals. Think of the miracles of science and technology: we can fly through the air; we can replace a failing heart. We can grow food in a desert.

We are great doers, even though it is equally true that we can be as destructive as we are creative.

But beyond all our doing, we act within a framework of a universe that is, for the most part, silent. Think for a moment beyond the confines of this noisy and busy planet. Image the vastness of space, the infinite reaches of fathomless silence.

Now draw that silence into yourself. Feel it. Allow yourself to float in it, weightless and calm. Feel it in your heart, in the very centre of your being.

This vastness, this peace that lies within you as much as it exists in the far reaches of the universe is where your true self resides. Here is the spark of God that animates you, and here is the door which, if you only knock, will open up to you and allow you to live your busy life – your 'doing' life – centred in the core of your being.

"Peace I leave with you; my peace I give to you. Not as the world gives do I give to you. Let not your hearts be troubled, neither let them be afraid."
John 14:27

If we are to find the peace that exists within us, we have to make decisions and live our lives by a set of rules that reflect the nature of how things are rather than the way we would like things to be.

The universe exists according to set of physical laws that are immutable, and when we learn to live in alignment with them, our lives will flow a little more easily.

The greatest universal law is love. This is not a sentimental attachment to particular people, places or things, it is a simple realisation that all of us, and everything that lives around us, are one life.

When we understand that the spark that animates us is to be found in the heart of every living creature, we begin to look at another's life with less judgement and more compassion, more empathy.

All beings struggle and suffer in their lives; all of us want peace and security, justice, warmth, clothing, food. We want to bring up our children knowing that they will grow into a world that will welcome and support and nurture them. The gifts of the spirit are not those of the world. Perhaps it is time for us all to give more time and attention to what we have within.

"A believer does not taunt, curse, abuse, or talk indecently."

Hadith, Tirmidhi

The process of becoming more at peace with ourselves and thus more effectively peaceful in the world is a slow one and a difficult one.

It feels natural, when we are under attack, to curse and mock our attacker. When we feel inferior in some way, we lash out, we fight back, we try to claim the superior position. We seek revenge rather than peace.

Peace sometimes requires that we look beyond what is being thrust upon us and make the effort to see where it is coming from. This does not imply a willingness to accept the attack or to overlook its seriousness. On the contrary, to consider, to think deeply, to respond with reason rather than with a reflex of righteous anger and defence at all costs – these things might just lead to a more favourable outcome for all.

We don't want a constant war, an eternal see-saw of attack and defence, right and wrong, us and them. We want peace, a peace based on mutual understanding. We want to remove the reason why someone would want to taunt and curse and abuse.

We want to be a blessing to the world and to be vehicles for the great blessing of peace.

"When a man's ways please the Lord, he makes even his enemies to be at peace with him."

Proverbs 16:7

The dream of a world at peace is one that has been part of our collective consciousness since the beginnings of civilisation. Even those who thought to 'impose' their peace on others saw their endgame as a settled – even if subjugated – world.

Nowadays, we understand that peace cannot be forced on a subject people; that peace is not simply a situation where violence and anger are subdued. We understand that peace must walk hand in hand with freedom and justice if it is to be real and lasting.

Knowing this, it is up to us to create a world in which these things can flourish. We have to start with ourselves, of course, and then look to our families and our communities; we have to be at peace ourselves and then let that peace spread out into the wider world.

Imagine a still lake. One raindrop falls in its centre. It creates a few ripples and it dies away. But imagine a rainstorm falling on that same lake. Its whole surface becomes an endless interplay of drops and ripples that interlink, again and again.

One peaceful person is a great and beautiful thing, but one is not enough. Let us determine to be a deluge of peace that floods the world, and whose spreading ripples never fade or die.

"...as members of one body you were called to peace."
Colossians 3:15

We simply cannot get away from the fact of our interconnectedness. Our spiritual teachings have told us of it for thousands of years and, today, even our scientists are finding that everything is entangled in ways that are still not yet fully understood.

This idea of oneness is the key that opens up the door of all spiritual understanding and knowledge. Beyond our individual bodies, minds, egos, there is an existence that we all share, and that implies that we are all affected by each other on some level.

Consider what this means for us: the illusions of separation and difference are the root of all conflict between us. "Me and mine" in a world of such marked inequality means that we feel we have something to defend and protect. But a world where everyone has what they need for a safe, happy fulfilled life is a world where we can all be happy and safe without needing to defend and protect.

The wheel of life turns inexorably and, whilst inequality exists on such a grand scale as now, those who are high will one day be brought low and those who sit at the lowest level of the wheel will rise. The cycle is clear; civilisations rise and fall. If we wish to break it, we must do it together, as one. Collective liberation must be our ultimate goal.

"It is Allah who is the ally of those who believe. He brings them out from darknesses into the light."
Quran 2:257

The key to finding peace within ourselves and in the world at large is to let go of the illusion of separateness, and to understand that all of our lives are entangled and connected.

Whether our understanding of the world is faith-based or not, we can still comprehend the concept that life is something that is present in all living things and that that life is the same in each of us.

For the believer, this idea may be easier to grasp but a believer who sees divergence from his or her particular set of beliefs as misguided and wrong, still has obstacles to overcome.

Mystics of all religions have managed to see beyond narrow dogma and are the closest in understanding. It is, perhaps, most profitable to seek out their teachings if we are still not clear.

But clarity is available to each one of us directly through our own lived experience. Just make time to sit quietly and go within. Ask for guidance; ask to know yourself; do the work that is needed to clear your heart of the detritus that material life has laid over it. Be patient; be persistent. Understanding will dawn; where there was darkness, there will be a light that will guide you for the rest of your days.

"Blessed are the peacemakers, for they shall be called sons of God."

Matthew 5:9

Our greatest task on earth is simply to be ourselves. It should be easy, but we live in a world of illusory forms that make it difficult to understand who and what we actually are. It's not that the world is false; of course not: it is real and beautiful and full of wonder. But it is a physical world and therefore all its outer life is temporary and constantly changing. This is why it is called illusory.

Our real life is eternal and exists beyond these outer forms. These bodies that we wear, which are so capable, so sophisticated, capable of feeling such a range of physical and emotional sensation, are also temporary and thus illusory. They are not 'us.'

Our reality is greater. It is almost beyond words to describe, but it is part of the great, eternal 'beingness' of the universe. We are spirit; we are love; we are peace itself and when we find our true selves and live in alignment with the truth of what we are, we automatically become manifestations of love and bringers of peace, because these things are our true nature.

And when we live in alignment with who and what we are, the universe naturally flows through us and we can rightfully claim such epithets as 'children of God.'

"For God is not a God of disorder but of peace."
1 Corinthians 14:33

Imagine for a moment the infinite reaches of space. Imagine floating in that vast silence. Imagine the peace.

Now think of the atoms that make up your body. They are more empty space than physical matter. Feel that spacious emptiness. Immerse yourself in the silence that fills those spaces. Imagine the innermost chambers of your heart, peaceful and at rest in infinite silence.

These moments of feeling the infinite within and around us; this touching of eternity: these are the moments where we can realise the truth of ourselves and of our closeness to God.

Here, within these physical frames, lies the secret of the universe: that beyond the world of forms there rests an eternal, unchanging beingness that upholds us and that is unlimited peace and rest and love.

This inner space is available to all of us at every moment if we only take the time to go within and find it.

To develop a daily practice of resting in this silent space is to allow ourselves to meet the seeming chaos, noise and busy-ness of our lives with a calm equilibrium, centred in the heart of our being.

"The believers are but brothers, so make settlement between your brothers."

Quran 49:10

Once we have begun to walk the spiritual path and our hearts are open to the possibility of eternity, we forge an indissoluble bond with other seekers. They become our fellow-travellers.

As we journey on our way, there may be stops and diversions. Some of us will take them. We might need a rest from the road. We might be distracted by entertainments and beauty spots: pleasant and interesting diversions along the way.

It is not for us to judge those who may become momentarily distracted from the great task of moving ever closer to our source in the Godhead. Nor should we accept the criticism of those who accuse us of stepping away from the 'true' path.

We are all travellers here; all moving at our own pace in the light of our individual preparedness for the next step, and then the next.

All seekers are moving towards the Light, even if they don't fully understand what it is yet. Our task is, at best, to encourage them and, at the least, to set them a positive example by joyfully treading our own path.

There should be no arguments about the way. We all have our own path to follow up the mountain. If we climb steadily, we will meet at the summit.

"He who teaches his neighbour's child Torah is regarded as if he had begotten him."
Talmud, Sanhedrin 19b

There is no doubt that we are born into particular situations in order to learn the lessons that will most help us progress on our path to enlightenment. The families we find ourselves a part of and the relationships that form as a result are our first classroom in the school of life.

As we grow, we find other connections: people who see the world as we do. If we are lucky, we find teachers, too: those who walk a similar path to us, but who may be a little further along it. We can learn from them and gain so much from the lessons they offer us.

And once we are consciously on a path to self-knowledge, we may be in a position to help others.

To learn in this way; to become more clearly and firmly centred in the truth of ourselves as spiritual beings: this is our greatest task.

Teaching and learning from others creates a sacred bond, stronger, sometimes, than the family ties that were our first support.

We are born into biological families but, as we grow and learn, we form networks of what we might call our logical families, within which we can continue the vital tasks of teaching and learning with open, receptive hearts.

"In Christ, we who are many form one body, and each member belongs to all the others."

Romans 12:5

We seekers of peace are united in a common bond of humanity. We aim to find solutions to conflicts that arise, both in our own hearts and out in the world, through means that constantly uphold the dignity and value of every life.

In mystical tradition, the concept of the Christ represents a manifestation or embodiment of God's love and so, while it is not necessary to identify as 'Christian,' it is possible to embrace this concept and help to bring God's peace to all people.

In love, all people are brought into a relationship of family bonds: we are all brothers and sisters, connected eternally and irrevocably in that embrace.

Those who consciously accept this relationship find great joy in understanding their connection to all people, but they also take upon themselves a great burden of responsibility. Once we know that we are brothers and sisters to all humankind, we must loosen the biological and cultural ties that birth or circumstance have thrust upon us, and begin to look for connections that go beyond the purely physical. It can be a hard and painful road, full of dangers and pitfalls, but the company is good and the destination is a paradise on earth.

"The believers in their mutual kindness, compassion, and sympathy are just like one body. When one of the limbs suffers, the whole body responds to it with wakefulness and fever."

Hadith, Sahih Bukhari

There is no doubt that the more things we have in common with others, the closer we feel to them and the more able we are to relate to them. Whether it is simply that we went to the same school or support the same team; or if we follow the same religion; are born into the same cultural or ethnic group; if we come from the same place: all of these things give us points of contact. The familiar is comfortable and we feel most at home with 'our own.'

But all of these factors are material. Even our religious allegiances are based on outer forms rather than inner truths.

The fact is that all people are 'our' people. We share a common humanity in the outer world and a common spiritual source in the inner. We are one people: this is the truth. Everything and anything that affects others resonates in us; and everything that we feel and experience resonates in others. Of course, we do not always feel it or know it, but it is the case nevertheless. Our lives are entangled, physically and spiritually. Surely it is time for us live in the light of this great truth.

"And if your brother becomes poor, and cannot maintain himself with you, you shall support him as though he were a stranger and a sojourner, and he shall live with you."

Leviticus 25:35

We set up boundaries to determine who are 'our' people and who are outsiders, but the vagaries of life often cause us to re-evaluate who stands where in relation to our current understanding. 'Us and them' seem fairly straightforward concepts but fortune's wheel can spin shockingly fast, and those whom we thought were 'them' can suddenly become 'us' and vice versa.

The truth is, of course, that the stranger is as much a part of us as is our nearest family; we just find that difficult to see, and those who are closest to us can drift away in time as paths diverge and each follows his or her own destiny.

We need to learn to see everybody as one. We need to learn to understand that all are equally worthy of our care and attention, whether they appear outwardly similar to us or not.

The life that exists in every person's core is the same life that exists in ours. The question of how much care we take over them should not be answered in relation to how 'close' we are to them, but solely in relation to our resources and abilities, and, of course, their needs.

"By this everyone will know that you are my disciples, if you love one another."

John 13:35

Knowledge is a wonderful thing and to be free to study and pursue one's interests without censorship or interference is a great gift and a measure of a peaceful, secure society. It is said that knowledge is power but it is also said that power corrupts. Self-knowledge has the capacity to bestow power but it, too, can lead to arrogance, egotism, delusions of importance and superiority over others.

True knowledge leads to an understanding of how much is still to be learned. True self-knowledge leads to an understanding of the oneness of life and this, in turn, leads to humility and then to a love that sees and accepts that the weaknesses and frailties that we see in others are also present in ourselves.

The truly wise person is not just a fount of knowledge, but also of compassion and understanding of what it is to be human. Cleverness is not a virtue in and of itself; it so often leads to manipulation and self-aggrandizement, Many of the things admired by our societies are worthless in the long run: the pursuit of wealth; the lure of physical beauty. None of these things will help us along the quiet paths of the soul.

The sign of the spiritual adept is not knowledge, or power. It is love.

"And hold firmly to the rope of Allah all together and do not become divided."

Quran 3:103

We have the ability to make the decisions that will lead to our collective comfort and peace. We have the means and the technology but we seem to lack the will. There is a clear divide between what the people want and what their leaders are willing or able to provide.

Whilst powerful people profit from war and agribusiness; whilst others are prevented from using land in ways that gives them affordable housing and meaningful livelihoods; whilst politicians shamelessly stoke fears of neighbour and stranger, and look to personal concerns before those of humankind, we are in serious trouble.

So what are the solutions? For each of us to hold on to our humanity; to work together in groups and communities; to create networks of support and mutual aid; to campaign for equity and peace in all our dealings with others, near and far; to educate ourselves and others on the truth of how things are; to be honest and open and loving.

If we are divided, we are weak. If we all pull in different directions, none of us will reach our destination. If we all pull in the same direction – towards peace and love and freedom – we will be unstoppable.

"Every blade of grass has its angel that bends over it and whispers, 'Grow, grow.'"

Talmud, Berakhot 33a

It's such a beautiful thought: that every living thing, however humble, should have its own guardian angel taking care of it. And yet, why not? Why not choose to live in a world where every life is precious and every life is accounted for? The very idea calls us towards reverence because all life is known by, and important to the spiritual powers that oversee us.

Even if it's not the literal truth – even if it's a metaphor – why not use it as a suggestion and a guide for how to live? We are all, every human being, embodiments of a Divine spark that resides within our hearts. Just to encompass that thought is life-changing in its profundity. And if we extend that to all life? How much more careful will we be with each other and our beautiful world? How much more respectful and loving?

Imagine, really imagine, that every person you see, every animal and plant that sustains our bodies or gives us joy, is accompanied by an invisible being of light – an angel – that is its hidden, higher self.

We can never go to war in this reality. We can never exploit and mistreat our fellow-creatures. This is a vision of the world that brings heaven down to earth; that creates for us a paradise of mutual care and unbounded love. Why not embrace it?

"We may have all come on different ships, but we're in the same boat now."
Martin Luther King Jr.

There are so many ways to live a life and so many individual realities. It may even be that every one of the seven billion human beings on this planet lives in a slightly different world, as their way of seeing things is formed by their unique experience and perspective.

Beyond these outer forms, though, it may also be that our consciousness rests in a vast ocean of being that is actually shared; that is one. So when we dream or meditate or pray, it may be that we attune ourselves to an inner reality that is the same, in essence, for us all. But we also bring our individual cultural programming to bear so that the way I experience or comprehend my connection with my inner life may be different from yours. A Buddhist might feel the touch of Nirvana; a Christian, the grace of Christ. So differences might remain and thus the potential for conflict still exists.

The way round this is practice. The more we learn to rest in this universal consciousness, the more we allow ourselves to sink into its truth, the more we will see that, eventually, we come to a place where the only reality is an eternal present. We are not Buddhist or Christian or Muslim or Jew. We simply are.

"The most complete gift of God is a life based on knowledge."

Hadith, Al-Bayhaqi

In a material universe, we have to accept that almost all of what we 'know' is based on observable facts relating to what is visible and physical and solid. We have instruments that help us see what is invisible to the naked eye and we can look into the far reaches of space, and into the world of the subatomic. And all such knowledge, if used wisely, helps us to understand and be more at home in our world. We develop understandings of who we are; our history; our cultural ties; our place in the order of things.

But, material knowledge does not necessarily bring us wisdom; does not make us better people; does not increase the aggregate of peace, justice and happiness in the world.

We also increasingly mistake opinion for knowledge and are daily bombarded with misinformation and 'fake news.'

It would be better if we put time into knowing ourselves; if we made the effort to look within and learned to abide in the field of consciousness which abides within our hearts. There lies the key to a different kind of knowing. Eternal and true, it will make us better people and it will bring peace, justice and joy to the world.

"You shall not hate your brother in your heart, but you shall reason frankly with your neighbour, lest you incur sin because of him."
Leviticus 19:17

All men are our brothers; all women are our sisters; all people are our neighbours. To allow communications between us to deteriorate to the point where we cannot speak to each other is to pave the way for misunderstandings. Misunderstandings lead to anger, anger to hatred and hatred to the severing of our bonds of brother- and sisterhood.

We are reasoning beings. Every time that we resort to violence, every time we feel anger or hurt rise up in us, is a result of the fact that we have failed to speak our feelings or to communicate clearly. This is as true on the national or international level as it is on the personal. Every war, every conflict, every bad feeling that arises between people, represents a lost opportunity to speak and listen deeply; a lost opportunity to feel and empathise; a lost opportunity to allow vulnerability and, thus, healing.

The skills we need to craft a world of peace and justice are present within us, but sometimes lie dormant and unused. We must begin to educate our children to uncover those skills, and we need to be willing to set aside aside the time to do the same for ourselves. It would be a sin not to do so.

"There is neither Jew nor Greek, there is neither slave nor free, there is no male and female, for you are all one in Christ Jesus."

Galatians 3:28

Again, if we consider the esoteric or mystical significance of the Christ as the embodiment of God's love, we can see that this quotation points clearly to the fact that beyond all physical or material considerations, we are one.

In spite of being separate entities, we share a commonality of spirit that means our every action, thought or word resonates in all other lives.

Sit with this idea for a moment. We have a connection that means, collectively, we can affect the lives of all. That means peace is within our grasp; justice is within our grasp; a life without fear and without lack is within our grasp.

The act of sitting quietly and of resting in the ocean of peace that abides within us, is not something we should do just for ourselves. It is not a selfish act, although it does bring great personal benefits. It is an act of service; a constructive act that helps to build a network of connection and positivity across the entire globe. Every block that is added to that structure helps us to erect a great spiritual edifice that offers shelter, safety and sanctuary to all beings. It lessens the aggregate of earthly suffering and offers all of us peace.

"Man was created alone to teach you that whoever destroys a single soul, it is as if he destroyed an entire world."

Talmud, Sanhedrin 37a

Imagine for a moment that every man is an Adam and every woman an Eve. Their story might be considered metaphorical or mythical, but it is not a stretch for the imagination to understand that every man and every woman is, potentially, the root of a multitude.

Jewish writings proclaim that to kill one person is to kill the multitude that they might have seeded or birthed, and so the admonition against killing – murder – is, and has always been, strong.

But this is not just about the possibility of breeding future generations. This is also about the here and now. Every human being has within them a spark of the Divine. Each one of us is connected and rooted in a great ocean of life and consciousness that is the world; that is the manifested universe; that is everything. To kill a person is to sever the link between the embodied soul and their current life, and to extinguish the light within that particular heart. It is like extinguishing a sun, and while we might believe that the soul continues, our interference in its progress is damaging to us and to the life we have interrupted. All life deserves reverence. Violence has to stop.

"We must learn to live together as brothers or perish together as fools."
Martin Luther King Jr.

It's easier to forgive someone who bumps into us accidentally than it is someone who does it on purpose. If we act in ignorance, we might be excused, at least once, but if we know something is wrong or detrimental to our well-being and we continue to do it anyway, that really does make us fools.

As a species we are endlessly engaged in destructive behaviour that we know causes us harm. We pollute the air we breathe, the earth we live on and the water we drink. We eat food that we know makes us obese and ill. We wage war on each other, we fight we steal, we kill.

And, meanwhile, we know what the outcomes of these behaviours will be: an over-heating planet, unfit for life; ill health, unhappiness, poverty, suffering. It is more than foolishness: it is madness. And it has to stop.

And it can stop, but it can only stop if we stop it ourselves. We can't wait for others to do it for us. It is within every person's power to find peace and live peaceably; it is within every person's power to reach out to neighbours, to say 'ours' instead of 'mine.'

We know what we need to thrive. Let's demand it: of ourselves, our neighbours and our leaders.

"You shall not oppress a hired worker who is poor and needy, whether he is one of your brothers or one of the sojourners who are in your land within your towns."
Deuteronomy 24:14

Everybody is worthy of respect and kindness. All of us are of equal value, embodying, as we do, the highest impulses that exist in the universe. We are divine sparks, made in the image of God. Not some of us: not members of a particular people or tribe or race: all of us.

Treating strangers or those in need badly does not reflect badly on them. They are not debased in any way by our oppression. They suffer, of course, as oppressed peoples have always suffered, but they are not lessened in any way by their oppression.

It is the oppressor who is debased, who, effectively, is saying that human beings are lowly creatures who can be mistreated and abused. There is no loss of dignity for a slave, even if he or she has lost everything else. It is the slave-owner whose dignity is gone: this person who thinks humans can be bought and sold like animals at auction.

We are brothers and sisters – all of us. As soon as we look down on another person, we lower ourselves. When we build someone up, we raise ourselves with them and move us all closer to heaven.

"And We have certainly created man, and We know what his soul whispers to him, and We are closer to him than [his] jugular vein."

Quran 50:16

If we listen carefully to the workings of our body, we can feel our heart beating; we can sense the blood moving, the diaphragm working, the flow of air pumping in and out of our lungs. If we take time to sit with these things for a little time every day, we can begin to feel ourselves, alive and present in this miraculous world.

If we listen harder; if we can, even for a few seconds, still the workings of our mind, we can hear or sense something beyond the bodily functions that animate us. Listen to them, but then go through them. Float on them and then let them carry you through to a place beyond heartbeats where an infinite ocean of peace awaits you.

It is in this state that we can hear the whispering of our souls. It is here that its voice urges us to rise up, to awaken, to see, at last, the truth of what we are and what, collectively, we could become. Between every heartbeat, between the rise and fall of every breath, lies the opportunity to connect with our deepest selves. It is there waiting for us to rest in its embrace, to listen to its truth, to come home.

"Judge the entire person favourably."

Pirkei Avot 1:6

It's very easy to make snap judgements based on limited knowledge. We make assumptions about people informed by the simplest, most surface of factors: the music they listen to, their political leanings, the clothes they wear, the car they drive; but these things tell us nothing about the entirety of that person.

Consider for a moment how difficult it is sometimes to even know yourself. Think how we struggle to find identity or understand our own motivations for what we do and feel. How much more difficult it must be to fully understand another.

Some people do terrible things, that is true. Some people do wonderful things. Most of us are somewhere in the middle trying to avoid doing the terrible things and striving for the wonderful.

Before we judge anyone, we should consider what they are: on one level, a human being just like us, trying to get on in the world and to make sense of it all. At the other end of the spectrum, they, like us, are an embodied soul, experiencing the world and learning its lessons as it seeks its home in God.

Life is messy. It has its ups and down, its failures and its successes. It is up to us to learn to stay balanced and centred as we navigate its tides. Everyone else is doing the same. Judge them kindly.

"Let us more and more insist on raising funds of love, of kindness, of understanding, of peace."
Mother Teresa

Charity is described as love in action, not just the giving of material support by way of money.

Money is useful, of course. In this world of ours where we need to buy money, clothes, shelter, medicines and more for those who suffer the hardships of poverty, disease and war, money is vital and those who give generously do a good thing. But charity is also giving of a broader, more human, more tender kind.

Charity is the listening ear, the gentling word, the encompassing arms. It is the open heart that feels what it is to suffer; the strong arm that determines to build something better. Charity is time spent with no thought of reward; it is sharing with a neighbour, a conversation with a stranger, a smile, a look, a nod of recognition.

We need charity of all kinds in this world at this time, but we should not lose sight of the fact that, if charity is still needed, it means that we as a species, for all our advancement, have not yet managed to relieve our brothers and sisters of their suffering. It means there is still work to do.

Money given as charity is vital to heal the wounds caused by our fractured world. Love given as charity is what will heal the world itself.

"The one who is not grateful to people is not grateful to Allah."

Hadith, Al-Tirmidhi

One of the things we try to do as we travel along our spiritual path is to train ourselves to see every human being as an embodiment of the Divine. This practice helps us act from our highest impulses of love, and it teaches us reverence and gratitude for the lessons that our fellow creatures offer us.

We don't have to believe in a personal God, running us like puppets, to understand that the universe has a tendency to place the things in our path that we most need to deal with. They come in many forms: as gifts, temptations, teachings, difficulties, conflicts, love and kindness, and a myriad other things that give us the opportunity to progress in our journey back to God.

And the vast majority of these opportunities are brought to us through the agency of others. It is through our interactions and relationships with other people that we learn and grow and come to know ourselves. From the families into which we are born to 'chance' encounters throughout our lives, we come up against these possibilities, the gifts of other embodied souls.

Even if God is not directly pulling our strings, the universe is so ordered that we attract what we need. For that, at least, we should be grateful.

"Do not be hard-hearted or tight-fisted toward your poor brother."

Deuteronomy 15:7

The values of the material world are such that we tend to look down on those who are poor, as if their poverty were the result of laziness or some kind of moral failing. At the same time, we honour and glorify those who accumulate and hoard wealth for its own sake, far beyond the needs of their entire lifetime.

How strange! What a clear and obvious sign that something is wrong. To hoard unneeded wealth while others starve: surely that is the morally questionable behaviour. Surely, that is the illness that we should be addressing.

Poverty has always existed, it is true, and yet, even now, there are countries and cultures that do not look down on it but which support and aid those in need. There are places where the turning of fortune's wheel is understood, and where the attitude is not, "These people are useless," but is more akin to, "But for God's grace, that could be me. I must help as much as I would wish to be helped."

To harden our hearts against those in need whilst looking up to those who, like mythological dragons, sleep on piles of gold, is to be infused with inverted values. It is to believe only in a material reality. It is to deny that great Unifier we call God.

"A new command I give you: Love one another. As I have loved you, so you must love one another."
John 13:34

One of the key differences between romantic love and spiritual love is the fact that romantic love carries a certain amount of need with it; it has a certain level of co-dependence built in to its structure. We behave in certain ways for desired outcomes. The love changes over time: it deepens if we are lucky and know what we are working towards. Sometimes it disappears when the passion that fuelled it is exhausted.

Spiritual love is not personal. It does not depend on what we do or how we are as people. God's love is available to us regardless of how we act. Even a murderer; even a hoarder of wealth who turns his or her back on the needy. God's love is there for them, but the truth is that until that love is returned in full measure, we cannot feel it and it cannot flow in our lives.

It is like an electrical socket: power is there, waiting for us, but our light will not illuminate until we put the plug in the socket.

This is the great secret: reciprocating God's love completes the circuit. Activate this love in any way that works for you. Meditation will do it, but so will a walk in the woods; so will the simplest act of kindness. To fall in love with creation is to love its creator, and then to discover that the universe loves you back!

"And man supplicates for evil as he supplicates for good, and man is ever hasty."

Quran 17:11

Discrimination on the spiritual path is one of the keys to progress. We need to be able to see clearly what will hinder our unfolding and what will support it. Then we need to choose the latter wisely and courageously, and step into the light we constantly glimpse ahead of us.

We know what is good for us. Whether we are talking about physical or mental health; whether we are talking about spiritual well-being; diet, alcohol, relationships, work, pleasure; whatever it is, we know.

And yet, we so often make choices that lead to negative outcomes. We choose what will not be good for us. We choose what will make us unhappy. We walk down paths that lead us away from what we really want and what we really need.

Happiness is a legitimate goal, but the ultimate goal is liberation, collective and personal. Actions which deepen inner happiness, which support physical and mental health, which add to the well-being of our communities; which cement relations between people; which encourage and support unity, peace, justice and love: these are the choices we need to be making. These are the sensible choices.

These choices are supplicating for good.

"A person should always be flexible like a reed and not rigid like a cedar."

Talmud, Taanit 20b

None of us has full control over our lives. We will all experience great joy and great sorrow, and everything in between, in the course of our time here on earth. We never know what the next moment will bring and so, rather than becoming victims of life's vagaries, we need to learn to ride its storms without being swept away.

If we can learn to be centred in the reality of our spiritual selves, we can train our minds to remain calm and free in the midst of the most tumultuous emotions. We can both feel and observe, and not become lost or overthrown. We can understand that our emotions are temporary; that they will pass and that we will remain. It doesn't mean we become unfeeling, it simply allows us to feel without attachment and drama.

We want to aim to let our feelings flow through us easily, like the wind through the trees. When the winds blow harder, we bow and bend before them without being uprooted. We do not resist because the storms of life are strong and if we do not bend, we might break or fall.

Firmly rooted in a sense of who and what we are, we can let the winds of life blow through us and round us without fear.

"The glory of God is man fully alive."
St. Irenaeus

Once we make the step to knowing ourselves to be spiritual beings inhabiting physical bodies, we begin to understand what the full potential of this human life might be.

Of course, we are animals too, and if we are not careful, that side of our nature can overwhelm us. But with training, through meditation, prayer or some daily practice of mental stillness, we can exercise control over our baser instincts and rise up to claim our birthright.

We are embodiments of the eternal divine principle. We are incarnations of love itself, we are pure, connected consciousness made flesh. We exist to manifest this truth on the physical plane: to raise up matter to the level of spirit through the power of love.

We don't need to do anything other than be the love that we are. We need peace? Love will give it to us. Justice? Love will provide it. Food and shelter for all? Health? Security? Home? Love can provide them all.

We don't need party politics. We don't need economic recovery plans; not unless and until they are motivated by love. Cleverness will not solve our problems. Love will. A fully alive human is one infused with love because, in love, we reflect God.

"The heart of an old person remains young in two respects: love for life and constant pursuit of acquiring knowledge."

Ibn Qudamah

We begin to age in our hearts when we 'fix' ourselves in terms of what we know and how we live. Once we stop seeking adventure, and retreat into a life of safety in the known, our world becomes smaller, more rigid, more confined. And when we become unable or unwilling to remain flexible in our world-view, in our political or religious beliefs; once we stop being open and alive to newness, we begin to atrophy.

In some ways it is understandable. The world moves so fast, and new knowledge and fresh ways of looking at things come at us everyday. It is not surprising that some people reach a point where they simply say, 'Stop. Enough.'

But stopping is not natural, and much of what appears new is, in fact, just a new perspective. One of the great movements forward of our times is that the formerly voiceless have begun to find their voice and to speak out. What they have to say may prick our conscience uncomfortably at times, but they also bring a great gift. They allow us to see the world anew, and thus to redress past wrongs, to restore balance; to be interested in the world again and stay young at heart, open to the excitement of change.

"Then the Lord God formed the man of dust from the ground and breathed into his nostrils the breath of life, and the man became a living creature."

Genesis 2:7

These bodies of ours are so wonderfully capable and complex, and yet so frail. They are all so different, yet they are all formed of the same elements – the same dust – and, in their time, they will all dissipate and dissolve back into the earth from which they came. This sense of temporariness, of mortality, the idea that we are here for such a brief moment and then gone again, this alone should make us want to seek peace and love and connection more than anything else.

Our lives are so brief! Why spend them unhappy or pursuing things that are, ultimately, meaningless. Why not spend them seeking happiness for ourselves and for our brothers and sisters?

Remember, too, that these bodies are not just bodies. They are animated by something that is not physical. The breath of God, the divine spark that shines in the depths of our heart, is everything that the body is not. It is immortal, undying, divine.

We share the same dual nature: we are, at the same time, weak, fallible humans and indomitable spiritual beings. If we can only live in remembrance of this, we will find compassion and, through that, we will come to live in peace.

"All that God created in His world, He created solely for His glory."
Midrash, Bereishit Rabbah 2:4

All of us are treading different paths, but we are all bound for the same destination. Our purpose on earth is to manifest the divine principle that lies within us. That means that we must first find the truth of ourselves and then acknowledge the truth of others, which is one and the same.

It is this simple act of self-realisation that will take us to where we want to go. This knowing of ourselves means that we must also know that the dead Gazan child is one of us; the kidnapped Israeli girl; the Houthi 'rebel'; the homeless drug addict; the transitioning man; the fleeing migrant; the neo-Nazi; the religious fundamentalist. All suffering, all extremism, all alienation are creations of an unjust, unbalanced world and all those who suffer or who cling to extreme views or who feel cut off from their society and community are us and a part of us, so it is up to us to create a just and fair world where everyone is free and comfortable to tread their own path without fear.

Human beings have the potential to crown and perfect life on earth. We have within us the ability to manifest and embody the highest principles. This is our function; this what we are for. Anything else is a failure and a falling short.

"Man is more himself, man is more manlike when joy is the fundamental thing in him, and grief the superficial."
G.K. Chesterton

It may not always feel like it, but our 'default setting' is one of contentment, of joy, of simply being enough. Beyond the chatter of our minds, buried by the traumas and neuroses of our upbringing, there lies a core of simple being that rests in an ocean of bliss.

It is so close to us, so easy to access, but if we look around us at the world we have created, where children starve or have to face bullets and bombs, the gulf between what we have and what we want seems insurmountable.

None of us can be truly at peace whilst others suffer. We can find the place of peace within us, but how can we stay there when so much in our world cries out for healing? So much is broken that individual liberation is not enough. Of course, we can only secure own liberation because that is an inner quest; but to be satisfied to live in a world where even the opportunity to sit in peace with a full stomach and a secure roof over their heads is denied to so many, is to live in a fool's paradise. It is like singing God's praises ever louder in order to drown out the cries of the suffering in the street. If joy is our birthright, we must secure it for all.

"Take account of yourselves before you are taken to account."

Hadith, Umar ibn Khattab

Beyond early childhood, every human being is responsible for his or her behaviour in this world and, because of the natural law of action and reaction, every act has its consequences. Our religions frame these consequences as punishments or rewards from a God who weighs and judges our everyday doings, but they can also be seen as the natural rebalancing that comes about because all life is one.

Our good deeds bear sweet fruit and our bad deeds condemn us. It may not always appear so: sometimes it looks like the 'bad guys' are winning, but that is purely a question of perspective. In the long run, the universe is a place of perfect equilibrium, operating on laws which we are still coming to understand, and it will, eventually, balance its books.

In the meantime, though, let's take responsibility for our actions because it is the adult thing to do. Let's act as if everything we do and say, even everything we think, has immediate consequences. What and how we are in the world is important. It changes things. If we wish to see a world of justice, peace and love, we have to create it. We have to understand that no-one else will do it for us. It is our responsibility.

"The Lord saw that the wickedness of man was great in the earth, and that every intention of the thoughts of his heart was only evil continually."

Genesis 6:5

Our animal nature is strong within us and our instinctual will to survive and thrive as individuals urges us, like wild beasts, to mark out our territory and protect it at all costs. We are too often ruled by fear. We close down our hearts; we shut our gates and bar our doors against the stranger, the 'other.'

This idea that we are all separate, that we can live happy fulfilled lives while others starve and suffer and die, is a great illusion. Our lives are inextricably bound up in each other's and so every thought or deed that erects barriers of exclusion and separateness hardens our hearts and moves us further away from what we are here to do and be.

We must learn to know ourselves: that is the first and most pressing of our tasks because in knowing ourselves, we come to see others for what they truly are and we come to understand our relationship with the Supreme Being we call by so many names.

If we knew there was treasure buried in our garden, we would make the effort to go out and dig it up. We have eternal treasure in our hearts. How is it that we do not seek it out? Is that not in itself a great evil?

"What good is it for someone to gain the whole world, yet forfeit their soul?"

Mark 8:36

The temptations of the material world are many and strong. We are constantly distracted by the desire to acquire new things: to reach for more money; more status; more power. The pit within us is bottomless because the more we try to fill it, the deeper it grows.

And the reason is simple: the longing that we feel within us for more cannot be satisfied with material things. Those of us who are lucky enough to have enough food, a safe place to sleep and the security to know that these things will continue to be, have a responsibility to make the world a better place for those who – to our shame – do not have access to those basic human necessities.

The hole within us is filled with acts of selfless service; with acts of love and kindness. It is filled when we recognise our relationship with others as one of mutual interdependence. The longing within us is not for things, but for connection: to ourselves, to others and to the world around us; to the great consciousness that binds us together as one.

We can lose ourselves in the pleasures of the world and they may give us the illusion of happiness for a time, but lasting joy, firmly rooted, is to be found in the gifts of the soul.

"Say, 'It is He who has produced you and made for you hearing and vision and hearts; little are you grateful.'"
Quran 67:23

These human bodies we inhabit are so wonderful. Think for a moment how they allow us to experience the world. Step outside. Look out and up. The smallest patch of grass, the endless blue of a clear sky, the infinite stretch of stars; the warmth of the sun on our skin. Every sensation is a miracle and a wonder. We are surrounded by such beauty, how can it be that our hearts are not constantly overflowing with gratitude?

And how is it that we have created a world where some cannot appreciate its beauty because they are hungry or ill? How is it that, for some, the patches of grass are buried beneath the rubble of bombed-out homes and the stars are only visible through the torn scraps of a makeshift shelter?

We all want to be happy; we want to make gratitude and appreciation a part of our daily practice. But being grateful for our own well-being is a limited blessing when we know that our brothers and sisters are suffering. Feeling grateful is part of the story, but until we start showing our gratitude by actively working to improve the lot of others, our gratitude is shallow and worthless: a squandering and a misappropriation of God's gifts.

"The world stands on three things: Torah, service to God, and acts of kindness."

Pirkei Avot 1:2

We can agree on these three things in principle, but until we can find consensus on what actually constitutes Torah, God's law, we will continue to experience division, conflict, war – all in His name.

So what is God's law? How should we be acting in this world to ensure that we are living as closely to our purpose as possible? How do we attune ourselves with the natural flow of the universe? How do we find a way to manifest the divine that dwells within us and create a heaven on earth?

If we are to serve God, if that is the second of the three pillars on which the world stands, how do we do so? Do we rid the world of unbelievers? Do we wage war on those who do not accept our Holy Book, or on those who do not think or act like us?

The answer to these questions lies in the third of these three pillars: acts of kindness. Love is the sum and total of God's law; it is through love that we learn to serve God's will, and it is through practical acts of loving kindness that we come to open our hearts and know that all people are brothers and sisters; that our God is one God, even if we know Him by many different names; that we are born to lift each other up in love, tolerance and peace.

"We are not human beings having a spiritual experience. We are spiritual beings having a human experience."

Pierre Teilhard de Chardin

This one fact is the most important piece of knowledge that we can have. It is the fundamental key to understanding what we are and what we are here for.

These bodies we inhabit are vehicles for consciousness and are miraculous in that they offer the possibility of full self-consciousness: they are the means by which the universe comes to know itself and evolve ever closer to its primary source.

To fully grasp this fact of what we are is not difficult. The truth of ourselves lies within us. It is close, between every heartbeat; in the space between each breath. We can all access it; it is our birthright; it is our centre, the truth and sum of our selves. It is the key to our continuation and immortality.

Our hardest task is to learn to still our mind. In this world of distraction and instant gratification, it is not easy, but if we can just practise the art of stillness, we can begin our quest. Through loving service, through acts of devotion to God and each other; through kindness, we can learn the taste of joy and, remembering it, we can know what it is that we seek. Our bodies can bring us great happiness, if we only learn to use them correctly.

"Do not waste your life in ease and comfort, but be ready for tiresome work and troubles. It is these which bring real happiness and peace of mind."
Imam al-Ghazali

It seems contradictory to say that we are made for joy but that we must be willing to undergo hardship. If we are meant to happy, why sadden ourselves with the troubles of the world?

The answer is that we must be clear about where true happiness lies. We must acknowledge that these are tumultuous times, but we can also understand that our great task is to face these troubled times and make them better. This is what we are for. This is why we have incarnated here and now. We are the ones who have taken on the responsibility to make the world a better, safer, happier place so this is what we must strive to do.

It is and will be difficult. There is so much heartache on the way; so much suffering to face and overcome. It can be overwhelming at times and we must learn to look to each other for help and support, and to look within for strength and guidance.

But we must also know that true, meaningful happiness lies in being perfectly attuned to our purpose and so, though the way is hard and steep and full of pitfalls, we walk it as best we can, with a quiet, inward joy, knowing that we are doing what it is we were born to do.

"The best way to defeat someone is to beat him at politeness."
Hadith, Al-Adab al-Mufrad

Imagine a world where we made heroes, not of the people who are the strongest or the richest or the most good looking, but of those who are good and considerate and kind. It's an amusing exercise in a way: imagine transfer fees of tens of millions of pounds changing hands for the best teachers, the most caring healthcare professionals or top fire-fighters. It's an entertaining thought, but it's not that funny as it highlights the truth that our value systems have gone seriously astray.

Kindness and caring are among the most important of virtues. They are the ones that make us truly human. Compassion, empathy, love: these are the attributes that we should be looking for and praising in ourselves as well as in each other.

If we must compete, it would be better if we tried to outdo each other in how well we foster fellow-feeling; how well we listen to each other's troubles and offer help; how effectively we promote and live by principles of love and justice.

We can distract ourselves with games and lose ourselves in our need to win, but these things are just distractions from the real business of learning to connect in love with our neighbours and our innermost selves.

"The Holy One, Blessed be He, is in need of a person's prayers, as it is said, 'And to Him who offers an offering in peace shall be the Lord's blessing.'"
Talmud, Berakhot 6b

When we offer something, to God or our fellows, out of a true sense of love and devotion, we align ourselves with the benevolent flow of the universe. Look how generous the earth is! Water flows, food grows, the sun shines, the rain falls. It is a miracle: the whole of creation supports and sustains us.

And yet we, with our great intelligence and technical know-how, are managing to upset the balance of nature; to create floods and deserts, drought, famine, sickness and war. It is as if we are separate from the forces that govern us; as if we were above them and beyond their reach.

But this is obviously not the case. We are a part of the universe; we are a part of nature. We have our place in the order of things and even if we consider our place to be at the 'top' of the evolutionary tree, it seems that we have badly misinterpreted what that means.

We are not despots, ruling creation through fear and aggression; we are Kings and Queens, who should guide and care for their subjects. We should rule in the old way, willing to make sacrifice for the common good. The world needs us; God needs us to take up our crowns and be a blessing to the world.

"For all have sinned and fall short of the glory of God."
Romans 3:23

To be human is to hold in our hands and hearts a complicated mess of emotion. We have a great longing to do something, but we don't know what it is; we aspire to great heights but we don't know how to reach them; we long for love and connection and a sense of peace but they seem so often to be out of reach like phantoms or ghosts, beyond our understanding.

To be human is to be flawed, to be imperfect, to make mistakes without fully knowing why; to turn away love; to misunderstand intentions; to quarrel and fight; to feel threatened; to know fear; to defend, to grasp and to hate.

And yet, to be human is also the opposite. It is to love and be kind; it is to heal hurts and bind up wounds; it is compassion, empathy and kindness. It is the gentle touch of a parent or a lover; it is the heartfelt gift, the act of generosity; it is charity; it is love.

Let us not dwell on our shortcomings. Let us not condemn ourselves or others for being less than we might be. Instead, let us take the time to find ourselves; to strengthen the best in ourselves and learn to live, actuated by our innate divine nature.

It may be true that we are all sinners, but we are all saints too. Shall we not begin to live as the latter and become mirrors that reflect the glory of God?

> *"The entire world is sustained for the sake of the breath of schoolchildren."*
>
> **Talmud, Shabbat 119b**

Our species stands at a great crossroads. There is so much wrong in the world, so much that might lead us to despair. Here we are, almost a quarter of the way through the 21st century and we are still facing war, hunger, racism and sexism as well as seemingly endless new forms of discrimination. Hatred finds ever fresh targets and ways to separate us.

And yet, quietly, in people's hearts, something else is growing. There is a spiritual revolution brewing. The idea that we are more than our bodies, that we are embodied souls is gaining ground. Scientists talk of a unified field of consciousness that confirms our interconnection. We are sick of war, of conflict of hate.

More and more we look for connection. We understand that we are strengthened by our common humanity, not threatened by it. People want to live in peace and comfort; people want a a just world; a fair world; a shared world. And if we want those things, we understand that we must be those things. We must live according to the values we espouse.

Our gift to ourselves and the generations that come after us – our children and theirs – should be and can be a world of happiness and plenty. It is in our power to make it so. Let's do it.

If you enjoyed this book and wish to support my work, please take the time to review it on the platform where you purchased it.

If you would like to and are able to help support me financially, or if you just want to find out more about me and my other books, please visit my website:

www.jontimarks.com

Thank-you.
Blessings of peace to you.